1

Did you know that Australia's First Nations People had contact long ago with people from other countries? This happened long before the First Fleet arrived. Sailing boats came from Asia and Europe. Very old Chinese and African coins have been found in Northern Australia.

2

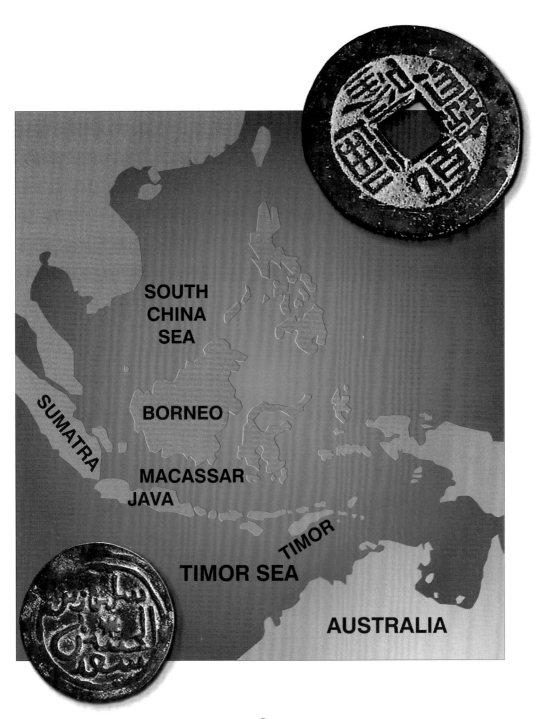

SOUTH
CHINA
SEA

SUMATRA

BORNEO

MACASSAR
JAVA

TIMOR

TIMOR SEA

AUSTRALIA

Knowledge Books and Software

Boats came from Indonesia to Australia. They came hundreds of years before Captain Cook arrived. These people were from an island called Sulawesi. They were called the Macassan people. They traded with our First Nations People.

5

The Macassans were very good sailors and fishers. They sailed to Australia in December to follow the winds. They returned to their island when the winds blew back towards Sulawesi.

Knowledge Books and Software

The Macassans traded with the First Peoples for the sea slug and use of their waters. The Macassans called the sea slug trepang. The trepang are used for food and medicine. They were smoked and dried by the Macassans and sold to people from China. Trepang is still a common food in China today.

Knowledge Books and Software

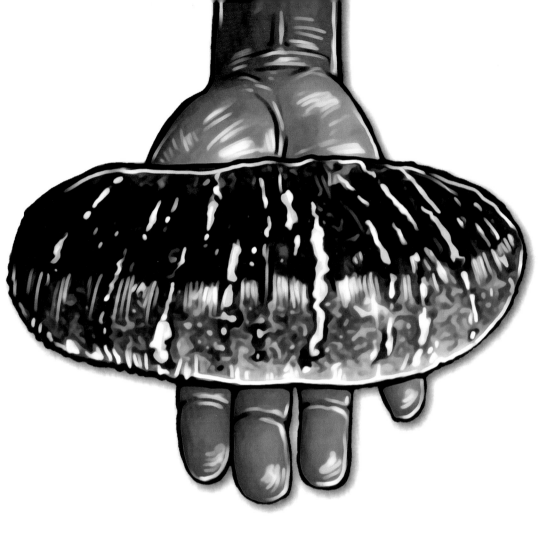

9

Trepang live on the coral sands. They eat small plants that grow on the coral. These plants are called algae. The trepang keeps the coral sands clean.

Knowledge Books and Software

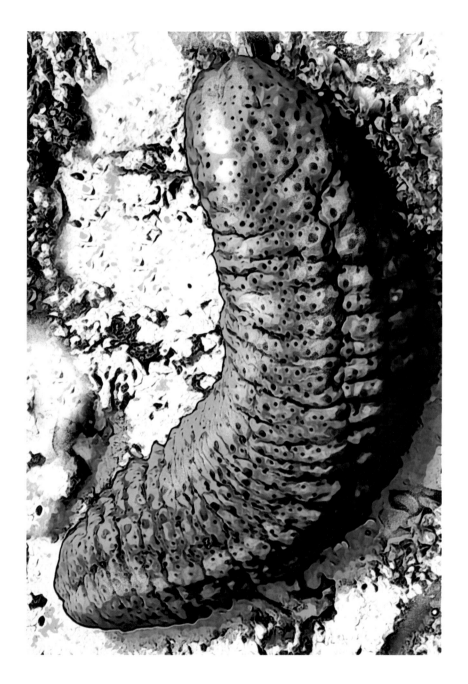

11

The trepang were taken and dried over fires. The dried trepang was then packed and taken back to Sulawesi.

Knowledge Books and Software

13

The Macassans lived for part of the year in Australia. Macassan graves and parts of their houses can still be found in Australia.

Knowledge Books and Software

The peoples of Northern Australia had worked with the Macassans. It is said that some First Peoples went back to Sulawesi. Some even went on to China.

Knowledge Books and Software

17

The Macassans lived peacefully beside the First Peoples. They shared some of their customs, songs, and dances with them. They even spread their faith to the First Peoples.

Knowledge Books and Software

19

The Macassans came to Australia for at least 400 years. They collected trepang and traded with the First Peoples. The Macassans were stopped from coming after Australia became a nation. The Red Flag dance of Arnhem Land is in memory of their sailboats.

Knowledge Books and Software

Knowledge Books and Software

Many people from other countries also visited Australia. Pearlers, sandalwood traders and Chinese explorers came. Dutch and Portuguese explorers also came from Europe. Australia was visited by many countries before the English settlers finally arrived.

23

Word bank

Macassan	Chinese	Portuguese
Indonesia	algae	Dutch
trepang	found	English
slug	customs	Arnhem Land
medicine	songs	
smoked	dances	
dried	nation	
Sulawesi	pearlers	
sailors	sandalwood	
Australia	explorers	

Knowledge Books and Software